# Anxious and Avoidant Attachment in Teens

Learn How to Recognize, Understand and Support Teengaers Attachment Struggles for Lasting Recovery, Healthier Relationships and Improved Mental Well-being

## Isaiah Air

# Table of Contents

# Introduction

Attachment theory, pioneered by John Bowlby in the mid-20th century, has revolutionized our understanding of human relationships, particularly in the crucial developmental stages of childhood and adolescence. At its core, attachment theory explores the bonds formed between infants and their caregivers and how these early relationships shape individuals' socio-emotional development throughout their lives. This introductory section will delve into the fundamentals of attachment theory, the different attachment styles, the significance of attachment in the teenage years, and the purpose of this book in addressing attachment struggles among adolescents.

## Understanding Attachment Theory

Attachment theory posits that the quality of early relationships, primarily between infants and their primary caregivers, lays the foundation for individuals' emotional and social development. According to Bowlby, the attachment behavioral system is biologically rooted, serving the evolutionary purpose of ensuring survival and protection. The theory emphasizes the importance of proximity-seeking behavior, secure base, and the caregiver's responsiveness in fostering a sense of security in the child.

## Overview of Attachment Styles

Attachment styles, as identified by Mary Ainsworth through her seminal research on the "Strange Situation" paradigm, encompass four primary categories: secure attachment, anxious attachment (also known as ambivalent attachment), avoidant attachment, and disorganized attachment.

- ☐ **Secure Attachment:** Children with secure attachment have caregivers who are consistently responsive to their needs, leading to feelings of safety and trust. They are comfortable exploring their environment, knowing that their caregiver will be there when needed.

- ☐ **Anxious Attachment:** Children with anxious attachment often have caregivers who are inconsistently responsive, leading to anxiety and preoccupation with their availability. They may cling to the caregiver and display distress when separated but have difficulty being soothed upon reunion.

- ☐ **Avoidant Attachment:** Children with avoidant attachment have caregivers who are emotionally distant or unresponsive, leading them to develop strategies to self-soothe and minimize their need for closeness. They may appear independent and avoid seeking comfort from their caregiver.

- ☐ **Disorganized Attachment:** This style arises from inconsistent or abusive caregiving, leading to contradictory behaviors such as seeking and avoiding proximity to the caregiver. Children with disorganized attachment may exhibit confused or fearful reactions.

## Importance of Attachment in Teenagers

During adolescence, attachment dynamics undergo significant shifts as teens strive for autonomy and form new relationships outside the family unit. However, the quality of attachment continues to play a pivotal role in shaping teenagers' emotional well-being, self-esteem, and social interactions. Secure attachment provides a foundation for healthy relationships, effective emotion regulation, and resilience in the face of stressors. Conversely, insecure attachment styles can contribute to a range of psychological and behavioral issues, including anxiety, depression, and difficulties in forming intimate connections.

# Purpose of the Book

The purpose of this book is to shed light on attachment struggles specifically experienced by teenagers and provide insights, strategies, and support for parents, caregivers, educators, mental health professionals, and adolescents themselves. By offering a comprehensive understanding of attachment theory and its application in adolescent development, this book aims to equip readers with the knowledge and tools necessary to recognize, address, and overcome attachment-related challenges. Through practical guidance, real-life examples, and evidence-based interventions, readers will learn how to foster secure attachment relationships, promote teenagers' mental well-being, and cultivate healthier, more fulfilling connections that endure beyond adolescence.

# Chapter 1

# An Overview of Attachment Theory

Attachment theory, a cornerstone of developmental psychology, provides valuable insights into the formation and dynamics of human relationships from infancy to adulthood. In this chapter, we will delve deeply into the origins and development of attachment theory, explore the four attachment styles, and examine their profound impact on teenagers' lives.

## Origins and Development of Attachment Theory

The roots of attachment theory can be traced back to the pioneering work of British psychologist John Bowlby in the 1950s. Bowlby, drawing on ethology, psychoanalysis, and developmental psychology, proposed that the early relationships between infants and their caregivers play a critical role in shaping the child's socio-emotional development. He argued that these early attachments are rooted in evolutionary principles, serving the adaptive function of ensuring the infant's survival and protection.

Bowlby's initial ideas were further refined through the groundbreaking research of Mary Ainsworth. Ainsworth's "Strange Situation" experiment provided empirical evidence for the existence of distinct attachment patterns and laid the groundwork for our understanding of the attachment system. Through careful observation of infants' responses to separations and reunions with their caregivers, Ainsworth identified three primary attachment styles: secure, anxious-ambivalent, and avoidant.

Over time, researchers expanded on Ainsworth's work, recognizing the need for a fourth attachment style: disorganized attachment. This style, characterized by contradictory behaviors and unresolved trauma, highlights the complexity of attachment dynamics and the importance of considering the caregiver's role in shaping the child's attachment experiences.

## The Four Attachment Styles

- ☐ **Secure Attachment:** Children with secure attachment have caregivers who are consistently responsive to their needs, providing comfort, and reassurance. These children use their caregiver as a secure base from which to explore the world, knowing that they can seek comfort and support when needed. In the "Strange Situation" experiment, securely attached infants may show mild distress upon separation from their caregiver but are easily soothed upon reunion. Secure attachment lays the foundation for healthy emotional development, resilience, and satisfying relationships throughout life.

- [ ] **Anxious Attachment:** Anxious attachment, also known as ambivalent attachment, arises when caregivers are inconsistently responsive to the child's needs, leading to feelings of uncertainty and insecurity. Children with anxious attachment may cling to their caregiver anxiously, fearing abandonment, but also display resistance and anger. In the "Strange Situation" experiment, these children may be hesitant to explore their environment and show intense distress upon separation, yet remain ambivalent or resistant when the caregiver returns. In adolescence, individuals with anxious attachment may struggle with low self-esteem, emotional volatility, and difficulties trusting others.

- [ ] **Avoidant Attachment:** Avoidant attachment develops when caregivers are emotionally distant or unresponsive, leading children to suppress their attachment needs and develop self-soothing strategies. Children with avoidant attachment may appear independent and self-reliant, minimizing their need for closeness with their caregiver. In the "Strange Situation" experiment, they may show little distress upon separation and avoid seeking comfort upon reunion. In adolescence, this attachment style can manifest as a fear of dependence, emotional detachment, and a tendency to suppress emotions in relationships.

☐ **Disorganized Attachment:** Disorganized attachment results from inconsistent or abusive caregiving, leading children to develop contradictory behaviors such as seeking and avoiding proximity to the caregiver. Children with disorganized attachment may exhibit confusion, fearfulness, or disorientation in their interactions. In the "Strange Situation" experiment, they may display disorganized or erratic behaviors, such as freezing or approaching the caregiver with apprehension. Disorganized attachment is often associated with unresolved trauma or disruptions in caregiving and can have profound implications for teenagers' emotional regulation, social relationships, and mental health.

# Impact of Attachment Styles on Teenagers

The attachment styles formed in early childhood continue to influence individuals' thoughts, feelings, and behaviors throughout adolescence and beyond. Adolescence is a period of significant growth and change, marked by the transition from childhood to adulthood and the emergence of new social roles and responsibilities. During this time, the quality of attachment experiences can have a profound impact on teenagers' emotional well-being, social interactions, and overall development.

Teenagers with secure attachment tend to have higher levels of self-esteem, better social skills, and more satisfying relationships with peers and romantic partners. They are also more resilient in the face of stress and adversity, able to seek support from others effectively. Securely attached teenagers feel confident in themselves and their relationships, allowing them to navigate the challenges of adolescence with greater ease and confidence.

Conversely, teenagers with insecure attachment styles may face a range of challenges that can hinder their development and well-being. Those with anxious attachment may struggle with self-doubt, clinginess, and fear of rejection, leading to difficulties in forming healthy relationships and asserting themselves in social situations. Avoidantly attached teenagers may have difficulty expressing their emotions, maintaining close connections, and relying on others for support, which can lead to feelings of loneliness and isolation.

Disorganized attachment in adolescence may manifest as emotional dysregulation, impulsivity, and difficulties in trusting others. Teenagers with disorganized attachment may struggle to regulate their emotions and behavior, leading to conflicts in relationships and challenges in academic and social settings. They may also be at greater risk for mental health issues such as depression, anxiety, and post-traumatic stress disorder, especially if their attachment disruptions stem from past trauma or abuse.

The impact of attachment styles on teenagers extends beyond individual well-being to influence broader social dynamics, including peer relationships, academic achievement, and future life outcomes. Adolescents who feel secure and supported in their relationships are better equipped to navigate the complexities of adolescence and emerge with a strong sense of self and healthy coping strategies. Conversely, those who struggle with insecure attachment may experience persistent feelings of loneliness, anxiety, and low self-worth, which can have long-term consequences for their mental health and future relationships.

# Chapter 2

# Recognizing Anxious and Avoidant Attachment in Teens

Understanding and recognizing anxious and avoidant attachment in teenagers is crucial for providing appropriate support and intervention. These attachment styles can profoundly influence adolescents' behavior, emotions, and relationships.

## Signs and Symptoms of Anxious Attachment

Teenagers with anxious attachment often exhibit a range of behaviors and emotional responses that reflect their underlying fear of abandonment and insecurity in relationships. They may demonstrate overdependence on others, constantly seeking reassurance and validation from peers or romantic partners. This overdependence can stem from a deep-seated fear of rejection and abandonment, leading to clinginess and a reluctance to be alone.

Emotional intensity is another hallmark of anxious attachment in teens. They may experience frequent mood swings, intense jealousy, and fear of losing relationships, which can dominate their thoughts and behaviors. Even minor disagreements or perceived signs of disinterest from their peers or partners can trigger feelings of anxiety and distress.

Teens with anxious attachment may also have difficulty trusting others fully. They may struggle to believe that they are worthy of love and may fear that others will eventually leave them. This fear of rejection can lead to hypersensitivity to any signs of disinterest or distance in relationships, further exacerbating their anxiety.

Furthermore, anxious teens may become preoccupied with their relationships, spending an excessive amount of time analyzing interactions and seeking reassurance from others. This preoccupation can interfere with other aspects of their lives, such as schoolwork or hobbies, as they prioritize maintaining their relationships above all else.

Overall, the signs and symptoms of anxious attachment in teenagers include emotional volatility, overdependence on others, fear of rejection, difficulty trusting, and preoccupation with relationships. These adolescents may experience significant distress and impairment in their daily functioning if their attachment needs are not adequately addressed.

## Signs and Symptoms of Avoidant Attachment

In contrast to anxious attachment, avoidant attachment in teenagers is characterized by emotional distance, self-reliance, and a reluctance to depend on others for support or comfort. Some common signs and symptoms of avoidant attachment in teens include emotional detachment, difficulty expressing emotions, and a preference for solitude.

Avoidantly attached teenagers may appear emotionally distant or aloof in their relationships, preferring to keep their feelings and vulnerabilities hidden from others. They may downplay the importance of relationships or dismiss the need for emotional intimacy, viewing dependence on others as a sign of weakness. As a result, they may struggle to express their emotions openly or authentically, often minimizing or suppressing their feelings to avoid vulnerability or rejection.

These teens may actively seek solitude and independence, choosing to spend time alone rather than engaging in social activities or seeking support from others. They may have a limited social network and prefer solitary activities that allow them to maintain control over their environment and emotions.

Avoidantly attached teens may also have a deep-seated fear of intimacy and vulnerability in relationships, viewing closeness with others as a threat to their autonomy and self-image. As a result, they may avoid deepening emotional connections or forming long-term commitments, fearing that they will lose their independence or be hurt by others.

Furthermore, teens with avoidant attachment may prioritize their own needs and independence above those of others, leading them to be dismissive or indifferent to the needs and feelings of their peers or romantic partners. They may struggle to empathize with others or provide emotional support when needed, maintaining emotional distance as a means of self-protection.

Overall, the signs and symptoms of avoidant attachment in teenagers include emotional detachment, difficulty expressing emotions, preference for solitude, fear of intimacy, and dismissiveness of others' needs. These adolescents may appear self-sufficient on the surface but may struggle with feelings of loneliness, isolation, and a lack of emotional fulfillment in their relationships.

Common Behaviors and Patterns in Teenagers with Anxious and Avoidant Attachment Styles

While anxious and avoidant attachment styles manifest differently in teenagers, there are some common behaviors and patterns that may be observed in adolescents with these attachment orientations.

Both anxious and avoidant teens may avoid conflict or confrontation in their relationships, albeit for different reasons. Anxious teens may fear rejection or abandonment if they express their needs or assert themselves, while avoidant teens may seek to maintain emotional distance and avoid intimacy by avoiding conflict altogether.

Relationships with anxious and avoidant teenagers may be characterized by unpredictable patterns of closeness and distance. Anxious teens may oscillate between intense clinginess and emotional withdrawal, while avoidant teens may alternate between periods of emotional detachment and brief moments of intimacy.

Both anxious and avoidant teens may struggle with regulating their emotions effectively, albeit in different ways. Anxious teens may experience intense emotional highs and lows, with difficulty controlling their reactions to perceived threats or rejection. Avoidant teens may suppress or deny their emotions, leading to a sense of emotional numbness or detachment.

Despite their differences, both anxious and avoidant teens may rely heavily on external validation and approval to bolster their self-esteem and sense of self-worth. Anxious teens may seek constant reassurance and validation from others to alleviate their fears of rejection, while avoidant teens may derive their self-esteem from maintaining a facade of independence and self-sufficiency.

Both anxious and avoidant teens may struggle with setting and maintaining healthy boundaries in their relationships. Anxious teens may have difficulty asserting themselves or expressing their needs, fearing rejection or abandonment if they establish boundaries. Avoidant teens may resist intimacy or push others away if they perceive their boundaries as being threatened.

# Chapter 3

# Understanding the Causes of Attachment Struggles in Teens

Attachment struggles in teenagers can be attributed to various factors, including their early childhood experiences, parenting styles, trauma, and other environmental influences. Recognizing and comprehending these causes is essential for providing effective support and intervention to help teenagers navigate their attachment challenges and cultivate healthier relationships.

## Early Childhood Experiences and Attachment Formation

Early childhood experiences play a pivotal role in shaping attachment patterns that persist into adolescence and adulthood. During infancy, infants rely on their caregivers to meet their basic needs for safety, comfort, and emotional regulation. When caregivers consistently respond to their infants' cues with sensitivity and warmth, infants develop a secure attachment style characterized by trust, emotional resilience, and the ability to form healthy relationships.

Conversely, inconsistent or neglectful caregiving can lead to insecure attachment patterns, such as anxious or avoidant attachment. Infants whose caregivers are inconsistently responsive may develop anxious attachment, marked by a preoccupation with their caregiver's availability and fear of abandonment. Similarly, infants whose caregivers are emotionally distant or unresponsive may develop avoidant attachment, learning to suppress their attachment needs and rely on self-soothing strategies.

These early attachment patterns are established through repeated interactions between infants and caregivers and are influenced by various factors, including the quality of caregiving, the caregiver's own attachment history, and the infant's temperament. Infants who experience trauma or disruption in their early attachment relationships may develop disorganized attachment, characterized by contradictory behaviors and a lack of coherent attachment strategies.

## Influence of Parenting Styles

Parenting styles significantly impact the development of attachment in teenagers. Diana Baumrind identified four primary parenting styles: authoritative, authoritarian, permissive, and neglectful. Each style is associated with different patterns of attachment and can affect teenagers' emotional well-being and relationship dynamics.

Authoritative parents are responsive and nurturing while also setting clear and consistent boundaries. They provide emotional support and guidance, encouraging independence and autonomy in their teenagers. Adolescents raised by authoritative parents are more likely to develop secure attachment patterns, characterized by trust, self-confidence, and effective communication skills.

Authoritarian parents are strict and demanding, emphasizing obedience and discipline over warmth and empathy. They may use punishment and control to enforce compliance, leading to feelings of fear and resentment in their teenagers. Adolescents raised by authoritarian parents may develop anxious or avoidant attachment patterns, struggling with low self-esteem and difficulties expressing their emotions.

Permissive parents are indulgent and lenient, often avoiding confrontation and allowing their teenagers to make their own decisions without clear guidelines or consequences. While permissive parenting can foster independence and creativity, it may also lead to attachment struggles, as teenagers may feel insecure or overwhelmed by the lack of structure and support.

Neglectful parents are emotionally distant and uninvolved in their teenagers' lives, failing to meet their basic needs for care and support. Adolescents raised in neglectful environments may develop disorganized attachment patterns, experiencing confusion and instability in their relationships due to a lack of consistent caregiving.

In addition to parenting styles, the quality of parent-child relationships, communication patterns, and parental mental health can also impact attachment formation in teenagers. Positive parent-child relationships characterized by warmth, empathy, and open communication are associated with secure attachment, while negative or conflictual relationships may contribute to attachment struggles.

## Trauma and Attachment Disruptions

Traumatic experiences, such as abuse, neglect, or loss, can profoundly affect attachment formation in teenagers. Trauma disrupts the normal development of the attachment system, leading to insecure or disorganized attachment patterns and impairments in emotional regulation and interpersonal relationships.

Adolescents who have experienced trauma may exhibit a range of attachment-related symptoms, including hypervigilance, emotional dysregulation, and difficulties trusting others. They may struggle to form close relationships or maintain healthy boundaries, fearing vulnerability and intimacy due to past experiences of betrayal or harm.

Furthermore, trauma can impact the caregiver's ability to provide sensitive and responsive care, further exacerbating attachment struggles in teenagers. Caregivers who are themselves traumatized or overwhelmed by their own experiences may have difficulty meeting their teenagers' emotional needs, leading to disruptions in attachment and exacerbating the effects of trauma.

## Other Factors Contributing to Attachment Struggles in Teenagers

In addition to early childhood experiences, parenting styles, and trauma, several other factors can contribute to attachment struggles in teenagers.

Family dynamics, such as conflict, divorce, or other disruptions, can impact attachment relationships and teenagers' sense of security and stability. High levels of family conflict or inconsistent parenting practices may contribute to attachment struggles, particularly in adolescents who are already vulnerable due to other factors.

Peer relationships play a crucial role in teenagers' social and emotional development and can influence their attachment patterns. Adolescents who experience rejection or bullying from peers may develop anxious or avoidant attachment patterns, struggling with feelings of loneliness, isolation, and low self-esteem.

Cultural norms and societal expectations can shape teenagers' perceptions of attachment and influence their attachment behaviors. For example, in cultures that prioritize independence and self-reliance, teenagers may be encouraged to suppress their attachment needs and prioritize individual achievement over interpersonal relationships.

Mental health disorders, such as depression, anxiety, or post-traumatic stress disorder, can impact attachment formation and interpersonal relationships in teenagers. Adolescents with mental health issues may struggle to regulate their emotions, communicate effectively, and form secure attachments with others.

# Chapter 4

# Effects of Attachment Struggles on Teenagers' Mental Well-being

Attachment struggles during adolescence can deeply impact various aspects of teenagers' mental well-being, influencing their emotional regulation, self-esteem, relationships, academic performance, and social functioning.

## Emotional Regulation Challenges

Teenagers grappling with attachment struggles often face significant hurdles in regulating their emotions effectively. Those with anxious attachment may find themselves overwhelmed by intense emotions, experiencing heightened levels of anxiety, fear, and insecurity. These emotions can be triggered by perceived threats to their relationships or fears of abandonment, leading to frequent mood swings, emotional outbursts, and difficulties in managing stressors.

Conversely, teenagers with avoidant attachment may struggle with emotional numbness or detachment as a defensive mechanism to protect themselves from potential rejection or hurt. They may suppress their emotions, burying feelings of vulnerability or sadness, which can result in a sense of emotional emptiness and disconnection from others. Over time, these coping mechanisms may impede their ability to form deep, meaningful relationships and contribute to feelings of isolation.

Additionally, teenagers with disorganized attachment may experience extreme fluctuations in their emotional states, oscillating between intense emotional reactions and emotional shutdown. This inconsistency in emotional regulation can lead to confusion, impulsivity, and difficulties in maintaining stable relationships, as they may struggle to understand and express their emotions in a coherent manner.

In essence, attachment struggles can disrupt teenagers' ability to regulate their emotions effectively, impacting their mental well-being and interpersonal relationships.

## Low Self-Esteem and Self-Worth Issues

Attachment struggles can significantly influence teenagers' self-esteem and self-worth, contributing to feelings of inadequacy, insecurity, and self-doubt. Adolescents who have experienced inconsistent or neglectful caregiving may internalize negative beliefs about themselves, leading to a diminished sense of self-worth and a pervasive feeling of unworthiness.

Teenagers with anxious attachment may seek external validation and approval to bolster their self-esteem, relying on others' reassurance to alleviate their fears of rejection or abandonment. However, this reliance can be fragile and fleeting, leaving them vulnerable to fluctuations in their self-esteem based on others' opinions of them.

Similarly, teenagers with avoidant attachment may develop a defensive sense of self-reliance and independence as a means of protecting themselves from potential rejection or hurt. However, this facade of self-sufficiency may mask underlying feelings of inadequacy or unworthiness, leading to difficulties in forming genuine connections with others and fostering a sense of loneliness or alienation.

Moreover, teenagers with disorganized attachment may struggle with a fragmented sense of self, experiencing internal conflicts and confusion about their worth and identity. They may alternate between feelings of worthlessness and grandiosity, leading to unstable self-esteem and a lack of confidence in themselves and their abilities..

## Difficulty in Forming and Maintaining Relationships

Attachment struggles can present significant challenges in teenagers' ability to form and sustain healthy relationships with others. Adolescents with anxious attachment may exhibit clinginess, possessiveness, and jealousy in their relationships, constantly seeking reassurance and validation from their partners or friends. This behavior can be overwhelming for others and may lead to conflict or rejection, reinforcing their fears of abandonment.

Conversely, teenagers with avoidant attachment may struggle to establish intimate connections with others, prioritizing independence and self-sufficiency over emotional closeness. They may avoid commitment or vulnerability in relationships, fearing that dependence on others will compromise their autonomy or expose them to emotional hurt.

Furthermore, teenagers with disorganized attachment may experience difficulties in establishing trust and security in their relationships, fluctuating between moments of intense closeness and emotional withdrawal.

Their unpredictable behavior and unresolved attachment issues can create instability and conflict in their interpersonal interactions, making it challenging for them to maintain healthy, fulfilling relationships.

In addition, attachment struggles can impact teenagers' ability to communicate effectively and empathize with others, further complicating their relationships. They may struggle to express their needs and emotions authentically or may misinterpret others' intentions, leading to misunderstandings and conflict.

Overall, attachment struggles can hinder teenagers' ability to form secure, supportive relationships, contributing to feelings of loneliness, isolation, and emotional distress.

## Impact on Academic Performance and Social Functioning

Attachment struggles can also have significant ramifications on teenagers' academic performance and social functioning. Adolescents who struggle to regulate their emotions or maintain stable relationships may find it challenging to concentrate and engage in school, leading to academic underachievement and disengagement.

Teenagers with anxious attachment may experience heightened levels of stress and anxiety, making it difficult for them to focus and perform well academically. They may prioritize seeking validation and approval from peers over their academic responsibilities, which can negatively impact their grades and overall academic success.

Similarly, teenagers with avoidant attachment may adopt a passive or indifferent attitude towards school, viewing academic achievement as less important than maintaining their emotional independence. They may avoid seeking help or support from teachers or peers, fearing judgment or rejection, and may withdraw from social activities or extracurriculars that require interpersonal engagement.

Furthermore, attachment struggles can impact teenagers' social functioning and peer relationships. Adolescents who struggle to form secure attachments may have difficulty navigating social situations, making friends, and establishing a sense of belonging within their peer groups. They may experience feelings of alienation or exclusion, further exacerbating their attachment struggles and contributing to social withdrawal or isolation.

# Chapter 5

# Supporting Teenagers with Attachment Struggles

Supporting teenagers who are grappling with attachment struggles is vital for their emotional well-being and the cultivation of healthy relationships.

## Building Secure Attachment Relationships

Building secure attachment relationships with teenagers requires a multifaceted approach that prioritizes trust, emotional safety, open communication, and autonomy. Caregivers, educators, and mental health professionals play pivotal roles in fostering these secure attachments.

One key aspect of building secure attachments is providing consistent and sensitive care. Teenagers need to feel that their caregivers and other significant figures are reliable and responsive to their needs. By consistently meeting their emotional and physical needs, caregivers lay the foundation for a secure attachment bond.

Moreover, creating emotional safety within the relationship is crucial. Teenagers should feel comfortable expressing their thoughts, feelings, and concerns without fear of judgment or rejection. Caregivers and mentors can achieve this by actively listening, validating their experiences, and offering support and guidance as needed.

Encouraging open communication is also vital for building secure attachments. Teenagers need to feel that they can express themselves freely and be heard. Caregivers can facilitate this by creating an environment where teenagers feel safe sharing their thoughts and emotions, free from criticism or dismissal.

Additionally, promoting autonomy and independence within the context of a secure attachment relationship is essential. Teenagers should be encouraged to explore their interests, develop their skills, and assert their boundaries while feeling supported and respected by their caregivers and other significant figures in their lives.

# Therapeutic Approaches for Anxious and Avoidant Teens

Therapeutic interventions tailored to the specific needs of anxious and avoidant teens can be instrumental in helping them overcome attachment struggles and develop more secure relationships.

For teenagers with anxious attachment, interventions often focus on reducing anxiety, building self-esteem, and enhancing coping skills. Cognitive-behavioral therapy (CBT) techniques, such as cognitive restructuring and exposure therapy, can help anxious teens challenge negative thought patterns and develop more adaptive coping strategies for managing their fears and worries.

Mindfulness-based interventions can also be effective for anxious teens, helping them cultivate awareness of their thoughts and emotions without judgment and learn to respond to stressors in a more balanced and mindful way. Techniques such as deep breathing, meditation, and progressive muscle relaxation can help reduce anxiety and promote emotional regulation.

For teenagers with avoidant attachment, therapy approaches that focus on fostering emotional expression, building trust, and developing secure attachments may be more appropriate. Psychodynamic therapy, attachment-based therapy, and experiential therapies such as art therapy or play therapy can help avoidant teens explore their emotions, develop insight into their attachment patterns, and learn to trust and connect with others in a safe and supportive environment.

Group therapy or support groups can also be beneficial for both anxious and avoidant teens, providing opportunities for peer support, validation, and learning from others who are experiencing similar challenges. Group settings can help teenagers feel less alone in their struggles and provide a sense of belonging and connection with others who understand their experiences.

## Strategies for Parents, Teachers, and Caregivers

Parents, teachers, and caregivers play crucial roles in supporting teenagers with attachment struggles. There are several strategies they can employ to create a nurturing and supportive environment that promotes healthy attachment relationships:

Foster a secure base: Parents and caregivers can serve as a secure base from which teenagers can explore the world and develop independence. By providing consistent support, guidance, and encouragement, they can help teenagers feel safe and secure in their relationships.

.

- [ ] **Validate emotions:** It's essential for parents, teachers, and caregivers to validate teenagers' emotions and let them know that it's okay to feel what they're feeling. By acknowledging and accepting their emotions, adults can help teenagers feel understood and supported, which is essential for building secure attachments.

- [ ] **Set clear boundaries:** Setting clear and consistent boundaries helps teenagers feel safe and secure in their relationships. Boundaries provide structure and predictability, which are essential for building trust and fostering healthy attachment relationships.

- [ ] **Encourage autonomy:** While it's important to provide support and guidance, parents, teachers, and caregivers should also encourage teenagers to develop independence and make their own choices. Allowing teenagers to take on age-appropriate responsibilities and make decisions empowers them and strengthens their sense of self.

☐ **Practice active listening:** Adults should practice active listening when communicating with teenagers, giving them their full attention and validating their experiences. By listening without judgment and demonstrating empathy, adults can help teenagers feel valued and understood, which is essential for building secure attachments.

☐ **Seek support when needed:** If teenagers are struggling with attachment issues, it's essential for parents, teachers, and caregivers to seek support from mental health professionals or support groups. Professional guidance can provide valuable insights and strategies for supporting teenagers and fostering healthy attachment relationships.

## Creating a Supportive Environment for Teenagers

Creating a supportive environment for teenagers involves fostering a culture of empathy, understanding, and acceptance within families, schools, and communities.

In schools, educators can implement programs and initiatives that promote social-emotional learning and mental health awareness. Providing access to counseling services, peer support programs, and education about attachment and healthy relationships can equip teenagers with the skills and resources they need to navigate their emotions and relationships effectively.

Communities can also play a role in creating supportive environments for teenagers by providing access to recreational activities, support groups, and community resources. By fostering a sense of belonging and connection, communities can help teenagers feel supported and valued, reducing feelings of isolation and loneliness.

Additionally, creating a supportive family environment is essential for teenagers' well-being. Families can prioritize open communication, spend quality time together, and foster a sense of belonging and acceptance. By creating a safe and nurturing home environment, parents and caregivers can provide teenagers with the stability and support they need to thrive.

# Chapter 6

# Promoting Lasting Recovery and Healthier Relationships

Focusing on developing emotional intelligence and resilience, building trust and communication skills, healing from past trauma, and cultivating positive relationships are powerful systems for teenagers in overcoming their attachment challenges and fostering healthier, more fulfilling lives.

## Developing Emotional Intelligence and Resilience

Developing emotional intelligence and resilience is essential for teenagers who have experienced attachment struggles. Emotional intelligence refers to the ability to recognize, understand, and manage one's emotions effectively, while resilience is the capacity to bounce back from adversity and navigate life's challenges with strength and adaptability.

One way to promote emotional intelligence and resilience is through self-awareness and self-reflection. Teenagers can benefit from learning to identify and label their emotions, understand the triggers that evoke certain emotional responses, and recognize how their thoughts and behaviors influence their feelings. By developing a greater awareness of their emotions, teenagers can learn to regulate them more effectively and make healthier choices in their relationships and daily lives.

Additionally, teaching teenagers coping skills and stress management techniques can help them build resilience and navigate difficult situations more effectively. Techniques such as deep breathing, mindfulness meditation, and progressive muscle relaxation can help teenagers calm their minds and bodies in times of stress, enabling them to approach challenges with a clearer perspective and greater emotional stability.

Furthermore, promoting a growth mindset can foster resilience by encouraging teenagers to view setbacks and failures as opportunities for learning and growth rather than insurmountable obstacles. By teaching teenagers to reframe negative experiences in a positive light and focus on their strengths and abilities, we can help them develop the resilience needed to overcome adversity and thrive in the face of challenges.

In conclusion, developing emotional intelligence and resilience is essential for teenagers' lasting recovery from attachment struggles. By cultivating self-awareness, teaching coping skills, and promoting a growth mindset, we can empower teenagers to navigate life's ups and downs with confidence and resilience.

## Building Trust and Communication Skills

Building trust and communication skills is crucial for teenagers to form and maintain healthy relationships. Trust is the foundation of all meaningful connections, while effective communication is essential for expressing thoughts, feelings, and needs and resolving conflicts constructively.

One way to build trust is by being consistent and reliable in our actions and words. Teenagers need to feel that they can depend on others to follow through on their commitments, keep their promises, and be there for them when needed. By demonstrating reliability and consistency, we can build trust and strengthen our relationships with teenagers.

Open and honest communication is also essential for building trust and fostering healthy relationships. Teenagers need to feel comfortable expressing themselves and sharing their thoughts, feelings, and concerns without fear of judgment or rejection. Adults can facilitate this by creating a supportive and non-judgmental environment where teenagers feel heard and understood.

Active listening is a crucial component of effective communication. Adults should strive to listen attentively to teenagers, giving them their full attention and validating their experiences. By listening with empathy and understanding, adults can foster trust and demonstrate that they value and respect teenagers' perspectives.

Furthermore, teaching teenagers assertiveness skills can help them communicate their needs and boundaries effectively in their relationships. Assertiveness involves expressing oneself in a clear, direct, and respectful manner while also respecting the rights and boundaries of others. By teaching teenagers to assert themselves assertively, we can empower them to advocate for themselves and navigate their relationships with confidence and integrity.

In conclusion, building trust and communication skills is essential for promoting lasting recovery and healthier relationships for teenagers who have experienced attachment struggles. By fostering trust, promoting open and honest communication, and teaching assertiveness skills, we can empower teenagers to build strong, supportive relationships based on mutual respect and understanding.

## Healing from Past Trauma

Healing from past trauma is a critical aspect of promoting lasting recovery and healthier relationships for teenagers who have experienced attachment struggles. Traumatic experiences, such as abuse, neglect, or loss, can have profound effects on teenagers' mental and emotional well-being, impacting their ability to trust others, regulate their emotions, and form healthy relationships.

One approach to healing from past trauma is through trauma-informed therapy. Trauma-informed therapy focuses on creating a safe and supportive environment where teenagers can explore their experiences, process their emotions, and develop coping skills to manage their trauma symptoms effectively. Therapeutic techniques such as cognitive-behavioral therapy (CBT), eye movement desensitization and reprocessing (EMDR), and somatic experiencing can be particularly beneficial for teenagers who have experienced trauma.

In addition to therapy, support from caring adults and peers can be instrumental in the healing process. Teenagers who have experienced trauma benefit from having supportive relationships with adults who can provide validation, empathy, and guidance as they navigate their healing journey. Peer support groups can also provide teenagers with a sense of belonging and understanding as they connect with others who have had similar experiences.

Self-care practices can also support teenagers in healing from past trauma. Engaging in activities such as exercise, mindfulness meditation, creative expression, and spending time in nature can help teenagers manage stress, regulate their emotions, and cultivate a sense of well-being and resilience.

In conclusion, healing from past trauma is essential for promoting lasting recovery and healthier relationships for teenagers who have experienced attachment struggles. Through trauma-informed therapy, support from caring adults and peers, and self-care practices, teenagers can heal from their trauma and build a brighter future.

# Cultivating Positive Relationships

Cultivating positive relationships is vital for teenagers' overall well-being and recovery from attachment struggles. Healthy relationships provide teenagers with support, validation, and a sense of belonging, helping them to feel valued and understood.

One way to cultivate positive relationships is by fostering a sense of connection and belonging within families, schools, and communities. Families can prioritize quality time together, engage in meaningful conversations, and create traditions and rituals that strengthen bonds and foster a sense of unity. Schools can implement programs and initiatives that promote inclusivity, empathy, and positive peer relationships, creating a supportive environment where teenagers feel accepted and valued.

Moreover, teaching teenagers healthy relationship skills can help them form and maintain positive connections with others. Skills such as active listening, empathy, conflict resolution, and boundary-setting are essential for navigating relationships effectively and resolving conflicts constructively. By teaching these skills, we can empower teenagers to build strong, supportive relationships based on mutual respect and understanding.

Additionally, encouraging teenagers to surround themselves with positive influences and supportive friends can enhance their well-being and recovery. Positive peer relationships provide teenagers with social support, validation, and a sense of belonging, which can help counteract the negative effects of attachment struggles and promote resilience.

# Chapter 7

# Improving Mental Well-being for Teenagers

Improving mental well-being is crucial for teenagers, especially those who have experienced attachment struggles.

## Self-Care Strategies for Teens

Self-care is essential for maintaining good mental health and well-being, especially for teenagers who may face unique stressors and challenges. Encouraging teens to prioritize self-care can help them manage stress, build resilience, and improve their overall quality of life.

One self-care strategy for teens is to prioritize sleep and establish a consistent sleep routine. Teenagers need adequate sleep to support their physical and mental health, so it's essential for them to aim for 8-10 hours of sleep per night. Establishing a regular bedtime and wake-up time, creating a relaxing bedtime routine, and avoiding screens before bed can help promote better sleep quality.

Engaging in regular physical activity is another important self-care strategy for teens. Exercise has been shown to reduce stress, improve mood, and boost overall well-being. Encouraging teens to find physical activities they enjoy, whether it's playing sports, going for a run, or practicing yoga, can help them stay active and improve their mental health.

Practicing mindfulness and relaxation techniques can also be beneficial for teens' mental well-being. Mindfulness activities such as deep breathing, meditation, and progressive muscle relaxation can help teens reduce stress, increase self-awareness, and improve their ability to cope with difficult emotions. Encouraging teens to incorporate these practices into their daily routine can promote better mental health.

Additionally, fostering healthy eating habits and nutrition is essential for teens' overall well-being. Encouraging them to eat a balanced diet rich in fruits, vegetables, whole grains, and lean proteins can support their physical and mental health. Limiting sugary snacks and drinks, caffeinated beverages, and processed foods can also help regulate mood and energy levels.

Furthermore, encouraging teens to engage in activities they enjoy and find fulfilling can contribute to their mental well-being. Whether it's pursuing hobbies, spending time with friends and family, or engaging in creative pursuits, providing opportunities for teens to engage in activities that bring them joy and fulfillment can help boost their mood and reduce stress.

## Seeking Professional Help and Therapy

Seeking professional help and therapy is an important step for teenagers who may be struggling with their mental health, including those who have experienced attachment struggles. Professional therapists and counselors can provide support, guidance, and evidence-based interventions to help teens overcome their challenges and improve their mental well-being.

One type of therapy commonly used to treat a variety of mental health issues in teenagers is cognitive-behavioral therapy (CBT). CBT helps teens identify and challenge negative thought patterns and develop healthier coping skills and behaviors. It can be particularly beneficial for teens struggling with anxiety, depression, trauma, and other mental health concerns.

Another effective therapy approach for teenagers is dialectical behavior therapy (DBT), which focuses on teaching teens mindfulness, emotion regulation, distress tolerance, and interpersonal effectiveness skills. DBT can help teens learn to manage intense emotions, improve their relationships, and cope more effectively with stressors.

For teens struggling with attachment issues and trauma, trauma-focused therapies such as eye movement desensitization and reprocessing (EMDR) and trauma-focused cognitive-behavioral therapy (TF-CBT) may be beneficial. These therapies help teens process traumatic experiences, reduce symptoms of post-traumatic stress disorder (PTSD), and develop healthier coping strategies.

In addition to individual therapy, group therapy can be valuable for teens, providing opportunities for peer support, validation, and learning from others who are experiencing similar challenges. Group therapy settings allow teens to share their experiences, practice social skills, and receive feedback and support from their peers under the guidance of a trained therapist.

It's important for parents and caregivers to support and encourage teens to seek professional help when needed. If a teenager is hesitant about therapy, parents can offer reassurance, normalize the experience of seeking help, and emphasize the benefits of therapy in improving mental well-being and overall quality of life.

# Addressing Co-occurring Mental Health Conditions

Teenagers who have experienced attachment struggles may be at increased risk for co-occurring mental health conditions such as anxiety, depression, substance abuse, and eating disorders.

Addressing these co-occurring conditions is essential for promoting lasting recovery and improving overall well-being.

For teens struggling with anxiety, therapy techniques such as exposure therapy, cognitive restructuring, and relaxation techniques can be effective in reducing symptoms and improving coping skills. Medication may also be prescribed in some cases to help manage severe anxiety symptoms.

Similarly, teens experiencing depression may benefit from therapy approaches such as CBT, interpersonal therapy (IPT), and behavioral activation. These therapies can help teens identify and challenge negative thought patterns, improve mood, and develop healthier coping strategies. Medication may also be prescribed to help alleviate symptoms of depression.

Substance abuse is another common issue among teenagers with attachment struggles, and it often co-occurs with other mental health conditions. Treatment for substance abuse may involve a combination of therapy, support groups, and medication-assisted treatment (MAT) for certain substances. It's important to address substance abuse issues promptly to prevent further harm and improve overall well-being.

Additionally, eating disorders such as anorexia nervosa, bulimia nervosa, and binge-eating disorder frequently co-occur with attachment struggles and other mental health conditions in teenagers. Treatment for eating disorders typically involves a multidisciplinary approach, including therapy, nutritional counseling, medical monitoring, and support groups.

It's essential for parents, caregivers, and mental health professionals to be vigilant for signs of co-occurring mental health conditions in teenagers and to address them promptly and comprehensively. By treating both the underlying attachment issues and any co-occurring mental health conditions, we can help teenagers achieve lasting recovery and improve their overall well-being.

# Finding Community and Peer Support

Finding community and peer support is an essential aspect of improving mental well-being for teenagers who have experienced attachment struggles. Connecting with others who have had similar experiences can provide validation, understanding, and a sense of belonging, which are crucial for recovery and healing.

One way for teenagers to find community and peer support is through support groups. There are support groups available for a wide range of issues, including attachment struggles, anxiety, depression, trauma, and more. These groups provide a safe space for teens to share their experiences, receive support and encouragement from others, and learn coping strategies from peers who have been through similar challenges.

Online communities and forums can also be valuable sources of support for teenagers, especially those who may not have access to in-person support groups in their area. Online communities provide opportunities for teens to connect with others from around the world, share resources and information, and receive support and encouragement from their peers. However, it's important for teenagers to exercise caution when participating in online communities and to ensure that they are engaging with reputable and supportive platforms.

Peer mentoring programs are another valuable resource for teenagers seeking support and guidance. These programs pair teens with older peers who have overcome similar challenges and can offer mentorship, encouragement, and practical advice. Peer mentors can serve as positive role models and provide valuable insights into navigating the challenges of adolescence.

Furthermore, participating in extracurricular activities and community organizations can help teenagers build social connections and find a sense of belonging. Whether it's joining a sports team, volunteering for a cause they care about, or participating in a club or hobby group, engaging in activities outside of school can provide opportunities for teens to meet new people and develop friendships based on shared interests.

For teenagers who have experienced attachment struggles, finding supportive relationships within their family and peer groups is especially important. Parents and caregivers can play a crucial role in supporting their teens' mental well-being by providing a safe and nurturing home environment, fostering open communication, and offering unconditional love and acceptance.

Similarly, friends and peers can provide valuable support and companionship for teenagers navigating attachment challenges. Encouraging teens to cultivate positive friendships with peers who are supportive, empathetic, and understanding can help them feel less isolated and more connected to others.

# Conclusion

In the journey of addressing attachment struggles among teenagers, it's crucial to conclude with a message of encouragement and hope for both teenagers themselves and those who support them. Despite the challenges they may face, there is reason to believe in the possibility of healing, growth, and resilience. Additionally, providing resources for further support and information is essential to ensure that individuals have access to the help they need beyond the pages of this book.

For teenagers grappling with attachment struggles, it's important to emphasize that they are not alone in their journey. While it may feel overwhelming at times, there is hope for healing and growth. Encouraging teenagers to recognize their strengths, resilience, and capacity for change can empower them to take steps towards improving their mental well-being and building healthier relationships.

One message of encouragement for teenagers is to remind them that their experiences do not define them. While attachment struggles may have shaped their past, they have the power to shape their future. By seeking support, practicing self-care, and cultivating positive relationships, teenagers can overcome their challenges and create a brighter tomorrow for themselves.

It's also essential to validate teenagers' emotions and experiences, letting them know that it's okay to feel the way they do and that they are worthy of love and support. Encouraging them to express their feelings, seek help when needed, and take small steps towards healing can instill a sense of hope and resilience.

For supporters of teenagers, whether parents, caregivers, educators, or mental health professionals, offering encouragement and support is paramount. Recognizing the progress that teenagers make, no matter how small, and celebrating their achievements can boost their confidence and motivation to continue on their journey of recovery.

Moreover, reminding supporters that their efforts make a difference in the lives of teenagers can provide encouragement and motivation to continue providing the necessary support and guidance. Building a strong support network around teenagers, including family, friends, and professionals, can ensure that they have the resources and encouragement they need to thrive.

Providing resources for further support and information ensures that teenagers and their supporters have access to the help they need beyond the pages of this book. Whether seeking therapy, connecting with online communities, or accessing support groups and peer mentoring programs, there are numerous resources available to assist individuals in their journey towards improved mental well-being and healthier relationships.

Addressing attachment struggles among teenagers is a complex and multifaceted process that requires understanding, support, and compassion from both teenagers themselves and their supporters. By recognizing the impact of attachment on mental well-being, providing strategies for building healthy relationships, and offering encouragement and hope for recovery, we can empower teenagers to overcome their challenges and thrive.

It's important to remember that healing is a journey, and progress may not always be linear. However, with patience, persistence, and support, teenagers can develop the resilience and skills they need to navigate their attachment struggles and build brighter futures.

By providing resources for further support and information, we can ensure that individuals have access to the help they need beyond the pages of this book.

Whether seeking therapy, connecting with support groups, or accessing online resources, there are numerous avenues for support and assistance available to teenagers and their supporters.

In closing, addressing attachment struggles among teenagers requires a collective effort from parents, caregivers, educators, mental health professionals, and the broader community. By working together and providing understanding, support, and resources, we can help teenagers overcome their attachment struggles and build fulfilling lives characterized by healthy relationships, resilience, and well-being.

www.ingramcontent.com/pod-product-compliance
Lightning Source LLC
Chambersburg PA
CBHW051847250726
48659CB00006B/2078